MERSA

written by: **Charlie Suero**

Illustrations by: **Carl Mefferd**

MERSA

Copyright © 2021 Charlie Suero

Illustrated by: Carl Mefferd • meffillustrations.com
Layout by: Darlene Swanson • van-garde.com

All rights reserved. No part of this publication may be reproduced, distributed, or transmitted in any form or by any means, including photocopying, recording, or other electronic or mechanical methods, without the prior written permission of the publisher, except in the case of brief quotations, embodied in critical reviews and certain other non-commercial uses permitted by copyright law.

For permission requests, write to the publisher at:
clsuero@outlook.com

First printing : 2021

ISBN:
978-1-7373977-0-0 (Hardback)
978-1-7373977-1-7 (Paperback)
978-1-7373977-2-4 (ebook)

Printed in the U.S.A.

This book is dedicated to
my loving grandmothers,
Merlyn McHardy
and Rosa Suero.

Hi! My name is Mersa, I'm as happy as I can be! I live in America with my beautiful family. However, there is a question that troubles me. My parents are from two different countries, so what does that make of me?

My father is from D.R.* (Dominican Republic) and my mother is from T.N.T* (Trinidad & Tobago).
I love them very much, and they love me!

My father likes to eat mangù* for breakfast, and rice and tòstones* for dinner. He loves playing dominoes with his friends and gets very excited when he is the winner! He also speaks Spanish, as that was the language he learned first. However, when I speak it, I think it sounds like the worst.

My mother likes to drink sorrel* and eat roti*, those are her top picks. She loves listening to soca* music while sweeping the floor with her broomstick. She's an amazing dancer and can do the limbo. However, when I try to do it, I look like a hippo.

Now, where does that leave me?

What if I like roti but I don't like sorrel?

What if I think mangu looks yucky but tastes very yummy?

I should ask my parents and see what they tell me.

"Hi mom and dad, I have a question for you, and this question has been troubling me, so I hope you can tell me what I should do."

Of course, darling what is it that you want to say?" asked mom.

"Please tell us so we can make your troubling question go away," said dad.

"I like to eat roti, but I don't like sorrel. I think mangu looks yucky but tastes very yummy! I can play dominoes with ease but have trouble dancing to Soca music with mommy. My question is, what does that make me?"

"Hee-hee, Ha-ha!" mom and dad, both chuckled.

"Is that the question that has caused you so much trouble? Well, listen carefully and listen close, this is the answer to your question and here it goes…"

"The truth is there is no one like you, Mersa. You are a unique individual just as the sky is blue. You are not defined by the music you like or the things you cannot do, but rather what you feel in your heart and what you believe to be true. Being a third culture kid can feel crazy at times. The most important thing to remember is to love yourself and you will be just fine!"

Glossary

1. Dominican Republic (D.R.): A country located in the Caribbean.

2. Trinidad and Tobago (T.N.T): A country located in the Caribbean.

3. Mangù: Mangú is a Dominican traditional dish. It can be served for breakfast, lunch, or dinner. Mangú is made up of boiled plantains or green bananas.

4. Tòstones: A Latin American dish of fried plantains.

5. Roti: A round flatbread.

6. Soca: A blend of calypso and soul music.

7. Sorrel drink: is dark red, a bit sour, with a raspberry-like flavor; made from the petals of sorrel plant; another word for sorrel is hibiscus (herb).

Special Thanks

To Carl Mefferd, Bianca Espinosa, Nicolas & Sun for helping to bring Mersa's story to life and bringing your creativity, love and passion to make this book a reality.

To Darlene for your patience, expertise, and honesty in putting this all together. Shanghai, China is a way long from sunny Florida.

All the educators and teacher's that make and continue to make a positive difference in each student that you come across.

CPSIA information can be obtained
at www.ICGtesting.com
Printed in the USA
BVHW091240050821
613728BV00008B/305